Ortho Easy-Step Books

Vegetables

*Created and designed
by the editorial staff of
Ortho Books*

Contents

Increasing the Harvest 47

More Information 54

Growing your own vegetables can be enjoyable for many reasons. You can save money, and you usually get better-tasting, fresher, and more nutritious vegetables than those available in supermarkets. You can experiment with different varieties, or grow large quantities of certain vegetables for canning or freezing. Some vegetable plants are wonderful for landscaping. A thriving vegetable garden is a source of pride, and working in it can relieve stress.

Beyond that, working in a vegetable garden—producing food from your own land in intimate contact with the soil—is an antidote for the toxins of modern civilization. With its engagement with living things and the basic processes of life in all their natural simplicity, gardening is the perfect balance to the impersonality and mechanization too often associated with modern life.

This book will guide you in planning a garden, preparing the soil, deciding what to plant, tending the garden, controlling pests and diseases, and harvesting and storing the vegetables.

Planning the Garden

Plan the site

You can grow vegetables in their own garden area or mix them with other landscaping. Pick a spot that gets at least six hours of sun a day, is sheltered from the wind, and has good soil that drains well. A convenient water source is needed. If only sloping land is available, use ground that slopes toward the south or southeast. Measure the garden area, then draw the dimensions on a piece of plain or graph paper. A 10-foot by 10-foot plot is a good size for a beginning gardener.

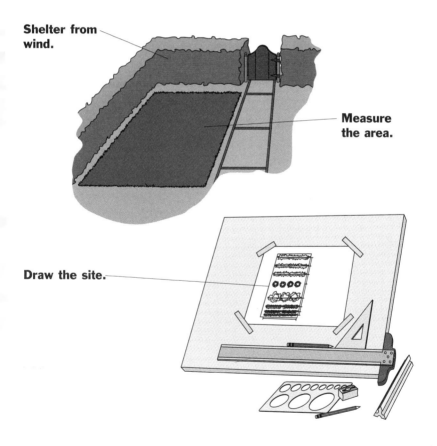

Shelter from wind.

Measure the area.

Draw the site.

Decide how to plant

Vegetables can be planted in *single rows* with a path between them wide enough for walking and carrying gardening tools. This method takes up the most space, and weeds can easily grow between the rows, but it is easy to work in. Use *wide-row* planting to increase yield without increasing the size of the garden. Individual plants may not be as productive as with single rows, but the yield will be greater for the area planted. Rows are 3 to 5 feet wide; the number of plants across the row depends on the type.

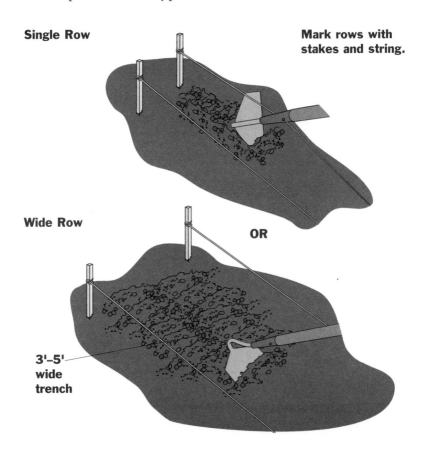

Single Row

Mark rows with stakes and string.

Wide Row

OR

3'–5' wide trench

Plant vegetables in raised beds for highest yields and where the native soil is poor. The beds can be simple mounds of soil, or they can have walls of wood or stone. Raised beds are at least 4 to 6 inches off the ground and up to 5 feet across. Their soil is dug deeply and often improved with amendments. In the spring, the soil dries out and warms up more quickly, allowing earlier planting.

Raised Beds

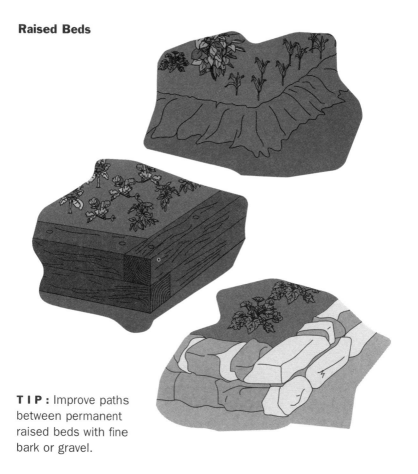

TIP: Improve paths between permanent raised beds with fine bark or gravel.

Choose your crops

Make a list of your favorite vegetables before deciding what to plant. Check seed packets, catalogs, and nursery transplant labels for answers to such questions as: Does the plant prefer cool or warm weather? How large do the plants grow? How many plants of each kind do you need? Consider how the plants are likely to do in your garden given its size, soil, and amount of sunlight. Check for frost resistance, hardiness, and the number of days until maturity (this is especially important in regions with short growing seasons).

Cool-Season and Warm-Season Vegetables

Distinctly cool-season crops that prefer 60° to 65° F, are intolerant of high summer temperatures above a monthly mean of about 70° to 75° F, and tolerate some frost.	Cabbage, kale, broccoli, cauliflower, turnips, rutabagas, kohlrabi, spinach, parsnips, lettuce, and celery
Crops adapted to a wide range of temperatures: Prefer 55° to 75° F and tolerate some frost.	Onions, beets, garlic, carrots, leeks, shallots, and potatoes
Prefer monthly means of 65° to 80° F and will not tolerate frost.	Muskmelons, cucumbers, squash, pumpkins, beans, tomatoes, peppers, and sweet corn
Distinctly warm-weather, long-season crops that prefer a temperature mean of about 70° F and tolerate no cool weather.	Watermelons, sweet potatoes, eggplant, some peppers, and okra
Perennial crops	Asparagus, globe artichokes, and rhubarb

Note: Cool-season plants are usually planted early in the spring and, in mild-climate areas, again in the fall. Warm-season crops should be planted after the last frost in the spring.

Whenever possible, use varieties that have a good reputation for flavor, resistance to insects and diseases, and ease of harvest (such as snap bean varieties that form pods at the top of the plant rather than the bottom). Consult local gardeners and nurseries. Consider how much time you are willing to spend harvesting, because some crops, such as corn and snap beans, need to be picked daily for peak quality. Crops such as lettuce, onions, and carrots mature more slowly, so you can wait several days between harvests.

Draw a final plan

Once you have determined the location and dimensions of your garden, sketch the area on plain paper or draw it to scale on graph paper. Fill in the plan, taking into account the space requirements (found on seed packets or transplant labels) of the crops you want to grow, whether you will plant rows or beds, and approximately how many plants you want of each type. Be sure to leave enough space between rows or beds for walking and maneuvering hoses and tools.

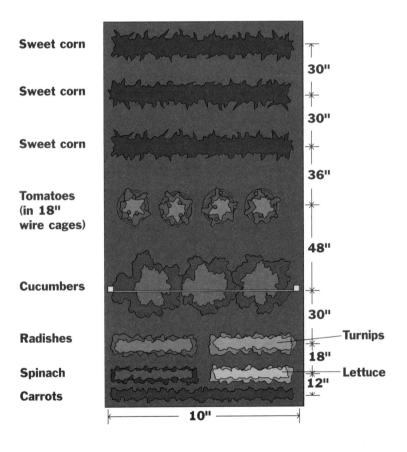

Sweet corn

30"

Sweet corn

30"

Sweet corn

36"

Tomatoes (in 18" wire cages)

48"

Cucumbers

30"

Radishes — Turnips
18"
Spinach — Lettuce
12"
Carrots

10"

Vegetable gardens are best oriented north to south, with the rows running east to west. The taller vegetables, such as corn, pole beans, and tomatoes, should be planted at the north end so they do not shade the lower-growing ones. This also gives all the plants an equal share of the noonday sun. If you want to grow perennial crops (those growing for a period of three years or more), such as rhubarb, asparagus, or artichokes, plant them along the east border, where they can grow undisturbed by yearly garden cultivation.

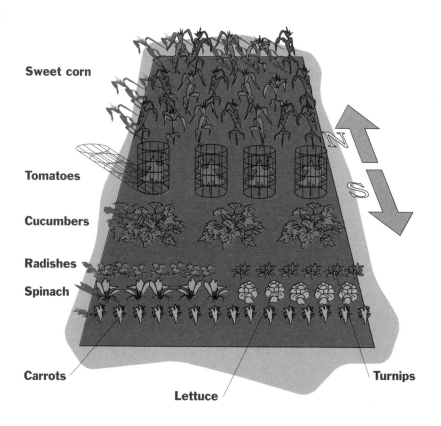

Sweet corn

Tomatoes

Cucumbers

Radishes

Spinach

Carrots

Lettuce

Turnips

Preparing for Planting

Test the soil

A routine soil test analyzes texture and measures pH (the level of acidity or alkalinity), nitrogen, phosphorus, and potassium. You can buy a simple, inexpensive soil kit and test the soil yourself. You can also have it tested by an independent laboratory. (Do this in the fall, when the labs are not as busy.) The written test results normally include ways to improve the soil—what amendments and fertilizers to add. Because soil conditions can change over time, retest the soil every three to four years.

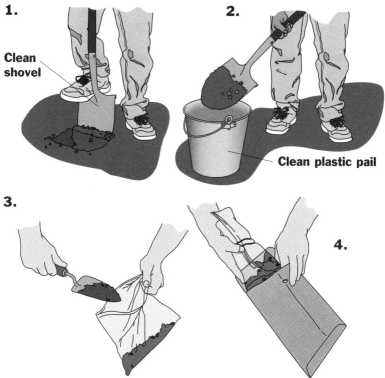

1. Discard first spadeful. Then make ½" to 1" cut about 7" deep.
2. Repeat process in other locations. Mix samples thoroughly.
3. Let soil dry completely. Seal 1 pint mixed soil in plastic bag.
4. Fold and secure bag with rubber band. Mail or take sample to lab.

2 Cultivate the soil

Whether preparing a new garden or readying the soil of an existing one, start by tilling the soil to a depth of at least 8 to 12 inches. Break up large clumps and remove any stones or debris. When using a rotary tiller, adjust the tines so that the first pass is fairly shallow. Set the tines to dig deeper with successive passes. Be sure the soil has dried out enough before working with it. Where possible, begin preparing the garden in the fall so it will be ready for planting earlier in the spring.

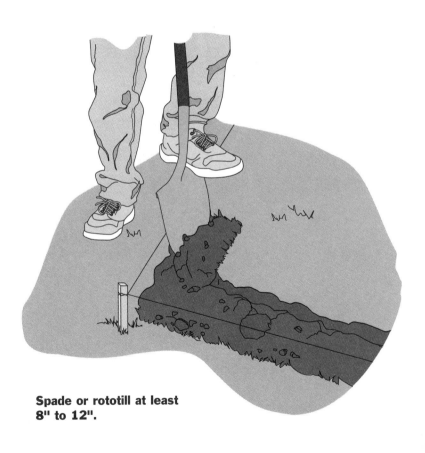

Spade or rototill at least 8" to 12".

Improve soil and ensure good crop growth with double-digging—digging the soil two shovel depths deep. Remove the soil one shovel blade deep along an entire row. Save this soil for later use. Turn over the soil in the bottom of the first row to the depth of the second shovel blade. Dig a second trench next to the first, filling the first trench with the soil you remove from the second. Turn over the soil in the bottom of the second trench. Repeat this process across the garden, using the soil from the first trench to fill the last one.

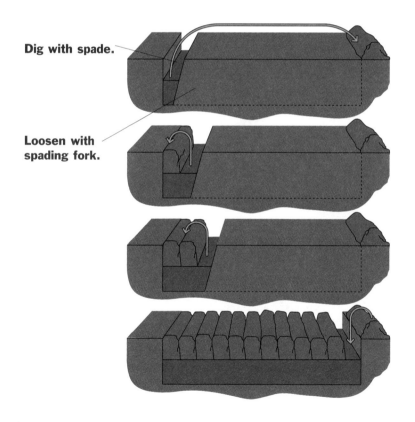

Dig with spade.

Loosen with spading fork.

Amend the soil

Adding amendments to soil improves its texture, structure, and workability. In sandy soil, use amendments to increase its moisture-holding capacity. Add enough organic matter, such as compost, manure, sawdust, or ground bark, to change the physical structure of the soil; at least a quarter to a third of the final mix should be organic matter. Spread a 2- to 4-inch layer of amendment on top of the freshly dug soil and work it in 6 to 8 inches deep.

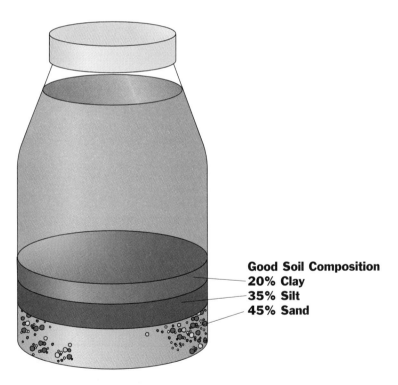

Good Soil Composition
20% Clay
35% Silt
45% Sand

Determine soil texture by filling a jar with two thirds water and one third soil. Shake, wait a few days, and note the layers.

If you add an amendment that is deficient in nitrogen, such as raw sawdust, ground bark, or straw, add a high-nitrogen fertilizer to help it decompose. If you have clay soil, add gypsum along with nitrolized (nitrogen has been added) sawdust, fir, or ground bark. Add amendments each time new crops are planted, as most of the amendments are used up by the previous crop. If the soil is so poor that it needs extensive (and expensive) amending, consider bringing in all new soil and/or planting in raised beds.

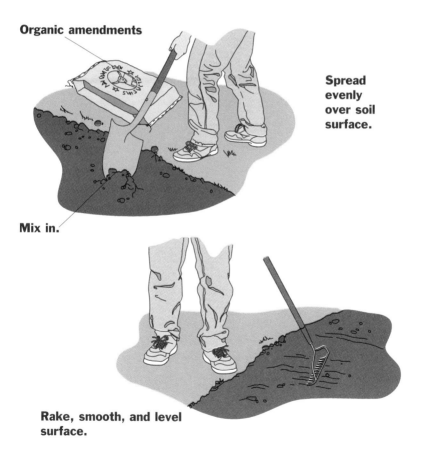

Organic amendments

Spread evenly over soil surface.

Mix in.

Rake, smooth, and level surface.

Prepare the planting beds

If you are laying out a garden for the first time, or are redesigning an existing one, measure the area carefully and mark the boundaries with stakes and string. Measure and mark the individual rows or beds as well. With wide-row planting, choose the width of the rows and run string along their outside edges to clearly designate the planting areas. Make raised beds by drawing soil from walkway areas onto the top of already loosened soil.

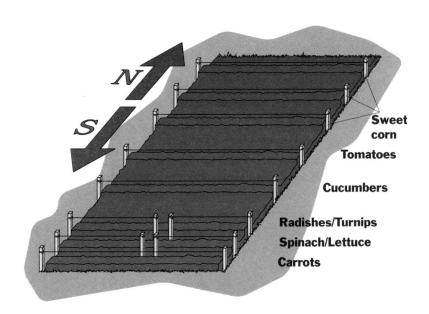

Sweet corn

Tomatoes

Cucumbers

Radishes/Turnips
Spinach/Lettuce
Carrots

Smooth out the soil and form rows or beds. Even after spading and tilling, the soil will probably still contain lumps and debris. Remove rocks and other materials and break up large clods with a garden rake. After one last leveling, you're ready to plant. The soil texture should be fine and crumbly, moist but not soggy. Do not walk over the area where you will be planting; stay in the pathways. Compacting the soil makes it difficult for seedlings to sprout as well as for both seedlings and transplants to send their small roots down into the soil.

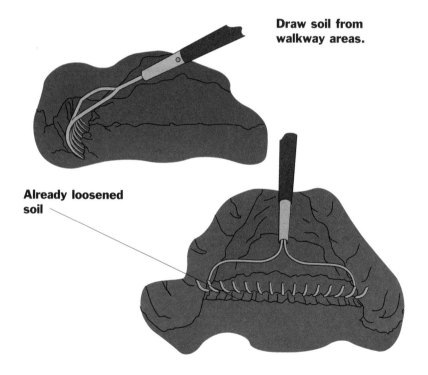

Draw soil from walkway areas.

Already loosened soil

Planting the Garden

Set up a record-keeping system

Keeping records helps ensure success with your current and future gardens. Record what was planted, how long the seeds took to germinate, how long the crop needed to mature, whether there was too much or too little to harvest, and what varieties did (or didn't do) well. Label all plants with the variety name and planting date, using white plastic labels and dark pencil or indelible ink. Keep your sketch of the garden in case any labels are lost. Also, seed packets are valuable information sources. Keep them for reference.

Crop (incl. variety	Date Planted Germinated Mature			Action	Results
Carrot (seeds)	5/20	6/3	7/31	Thinned 6/15	Add another row next year
Tomatoes (Transplants)	5/22	n/a	7/29	Fertilized 7/1	Plants were much greener
Squash (seeds)	5/22	6/2	7/20	Sprayed for mildew 7/1	Reduced mildew problem

Start seeds indoors . . .

Start indoors those crops that are difficult to sprout outdoors or that require a long growing season. To determine when seeds should be started, see the chart on pages 56 to 59 and count backward from the intended transplanting date. Moisten any fiber or peat containers. Plastic pots, egg cartons, or paper cups with holes in the bottom can also be used. For large numbers of seeds, use flats or trays. Sow seeds as instructed on the seed packet, and label them carefully. Cover with a thin layer of medium.

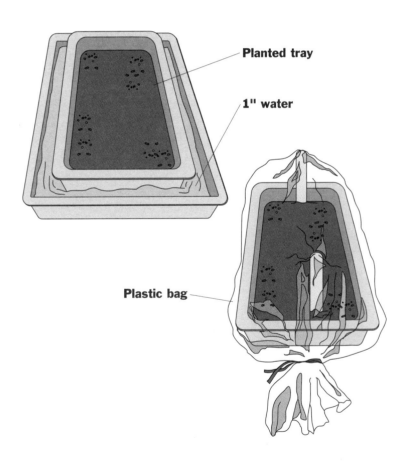

Planted tray

1" water

Plastic bag

Spray with a fine mist or set the containers in an inch of water, allowing it to seep upward to moisten the medium. Drain the containers and place them in clear plastic bags. Make small holes for ventilation, or open the bags for fifteen minutes each day. Put the containers out of direct sunlight where the temperature is 70° to 75° F. Keep the medium moist. When the seeds sprout, remove the bags and set the containers in a sunny window. Seeds sprouted in a tray can be transplanted to individual containers after the second set of leaves appears.

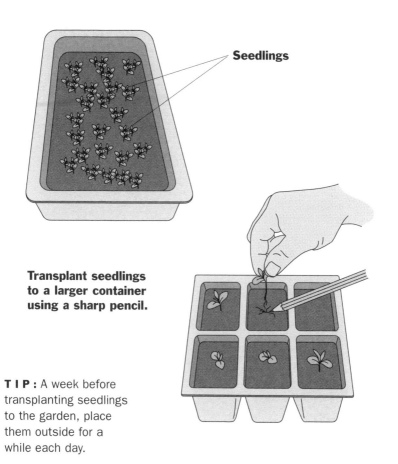

Seedlings

Transplant seedlings to a larger container using a sharp pencil.

T I P : A week before transplanting seedlings to the garden, place them outside for a while each day.

... or sow seeds in the garden

A few days before you sow seeds outside, moisten the soil thoroughly. Make shallow furrows in the prepared soil for single- or wide-row planting, or lightly cultivate the top of the soil on a raised bed. Sow small seeds thinly and evenly to the depth indicated on the seed packet by tapping the packet with your finger. For more uniform spacing, mix very small seed with sand or a light soil mix and then plant. Plant large seeds by hand. Seed tapes can also be used.

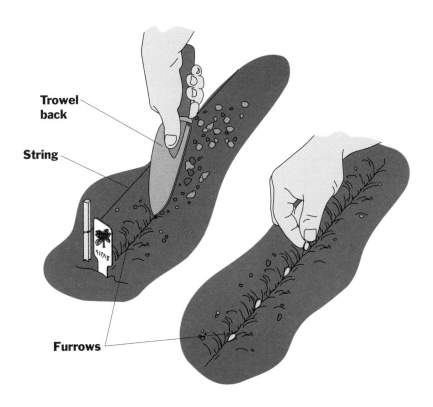

Trowel back

String

Furrows

Lightly cover the seeds and gently tamp the soil. Spray the seedbed with a fine mist, and do not let it dry out. After the seeds germinate, gradually reduce watering as the plants mature. Remove weeds carefully. When the seedlings are 2 to 3 inches tall, thin them according to instructions on the seed packet (or see the chart on pages 56 to 59). Thinnings can be carefully transplanted, given away, or, in some cases, eaten. You can also cut them off at the base of the stem with scissors to keep from damaging the roots of nearby plants.

To thin, cut stem base . . .

. . . or pull out carefully.

4 Set out transplants

Transplant seedlings you start indoors or healthy plants purchased from a reputable nursery. Moisten the garden soil and the transplants a day or so before planting. If possible, transplant late in the afternoon or on a cloudy day. If the transplants have been growing in flats, carefully cut out each plant with its rootball using a knife or trowel. If they are in individual pots or flats with compartments, turn the container upside down and tap gently on the bottom; they should come out easily.

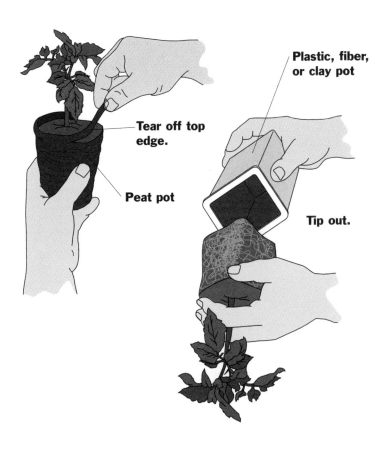

Tear off top edge.

Peat pot

Plastic, fiber, or clay pot

Tip out.

Dig a hole in the garden soil slightly larger than the rootball of the plant. Set the transplants to the same depth as they were in their container. Firm the soil around the rootball and water immediately. If necessary, protect the young plants from wind with a screen of plastic or burlap. Shade can be provided for a few days with one or two vertical pieces of wood. If a late frost threatens, cover the transplants with cloches as described on page 49, making sure they have proper ventilation.

Firm the soil.
Then water lightly.

Shade

Plant tubers, sets, and crowns

Potatoes can be planted as tubers, using certified disease-free seed potatoes. Plant them whole or cut them about 1½ inches square three or four days before planting, making sure each has at least one good growing eye. Set the pieces, eye up, cut side down, about 4 inches deep and 12 inches apart in rows 2 to 3 feet apart. Plant onions from sets (small dry onions available in late winter and early spring). Follow the planting instructions on the package. Asparagus is usually started with one-year-old crowns planted in late spring.

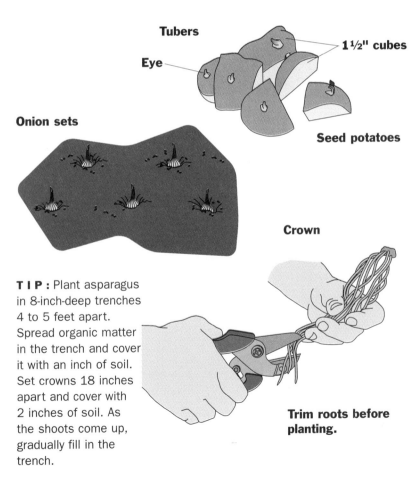

Tubers

Eye

1½" cubes

Onion sets

Seed potatoes

Crown

TIP : Plant asparagus in 8-inch-deep trenches 4 to 5 feet apart. Spread organic matter in the trench and cover it with an inch of soil. Set crowns 18 inches apart and cover with 2 inches of soil. As the shoots come up, gradually fill in the trench.

Trim roots before planting.

6 Plant in containers

Vegetables can be grown on decks, patios, or balconies in tubs, pots, and planter boxes of all shapes and sizes. The only essential is drainage.

Fill the container with a bagged planting mix, not garden soil (which will pack down with repeated watering). Keep the mix moist, and apply enough water each time so that some of it drains out. Fertilize with small amounts of controlled-release, granular, or liquid fertilizer. Compact or dwarf varieties are generally the best choice for containers.

T I P : Vegetables well adapted to containers include: short-rooted carrots, eggplant, kale, lettuce, onions, peas (with trellis), peppers, radishes, Swiss chard, tomatoes, watercress, bush-type beans, cucumbers, and summer squash.

Tending the Garden

Weed the garden

Pull weeds by hand or with a hoe as soon as they appear. Work in moist soil and be careful not to disturb the vegetables' roots. Mulch to help prevent weed growth (see page 38). Planting vegetables close to each other, resulting in a dense cover of leaves, reduces weed growth as well. To avoid damaging the crop, do not use chemical weed killers in a vegetable garden.

2 Water properly

Keep newly planted seeds and transplants moist until they are established. Water more mature plants thoroughly, allow the soil to dry out a bit, and, when needed, water again. Watering deeply encourages plant roots to grow well into the soil. The day after you've watered, you can dig down about 8 inches and see if the moisture penetrated. It is best to water in the morning when absorption is best and less water is lost to evaporation. Also, leaves will stay dryer at night, minimizing disease problems from dampness and cool temperatures.

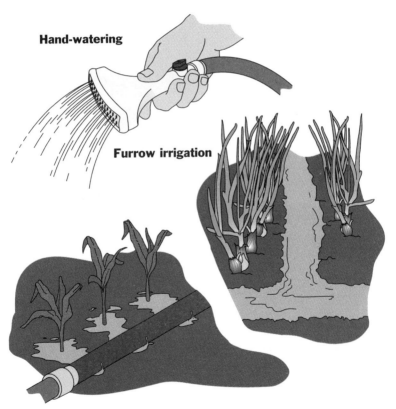

Hand-watering

Furrow irrigation

Drip system

Water small gardens by hand. For larger areas, use furrow irrigation, applying water slowly in a shallow, level ditch no more than 3 to 4 inches from each vegetable row. Drip emitter systems distribute water through outlets for individual plants or through a porous-hose system for rows of crops. Portable soaker hoses can be laid between rows, holes down for a deep soaking, or holes up for a fine spray. Underground or hose-end sprinklers spray water evenly over a larger area. Choose one with a spray pattern that matches your garden area.

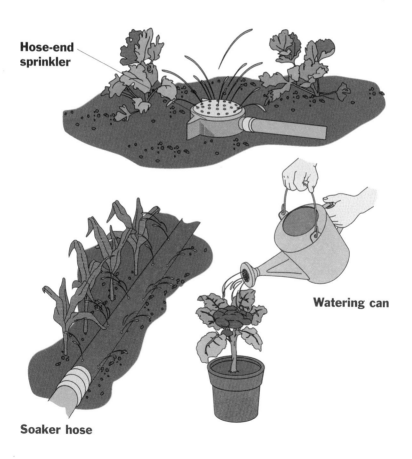

Hose-end sprinkler

Watering can

Soaker hose

Fertilize as needed

Fertilizer can be applied when the soil is first prepared for planting by digging in dry organic or inorganic types. Scatter a pre-plant fertilizer such as 10-15-10 (10 percent nitrogen, 15 percent phosphorus, 10 percent potassium) as evenly as possible over the bare ground with a handheld or mechanical push-type spreader. Dig or till into the soil 6 to 8 inches deep. Fertilizer labels specify the amount to apply in pounds per square feet of garden area. Read the label, then calculate the amount you should use based on the size of the garden.

Fertilizer Tips

- Be sparing with all types of fertilizers. Using too much can harm plants and might even kill them.
- Follow label directions.
- After applying dry fertilizer, water thoroughly to dissolve the fertilizer and carry it into the root zone.
- When using large amounts of fertilizer for such heavy feeders as corn, squash, and tomatoes, apply half the amount before planting, then side-dress with the remainder once growth is under way.
- Check the timing for applying fertilizer for each type of plant. Because fertilizer is beneficial to early vigorous leaf growth, the first application is often crucial.
- Give less nitrogen to plants grown in partial shade than to the same plants grown in full sun.
- Increase the amount of fertilizer when plants are crowded into narrowly spaced rows and when plants are grown in a random pattern in a small plot.

When the plants are established, dry fertilizer can be broad-cast over the soil surface, lightly scratched in, and watered thoroughly. (Be sure to wash any off the plant leaves.) A 5-10-10 fertilizer is a good choice for many crops. Another method is to make a shallow trench about 4 inches from the plants alongside the row (or in a ring around widely spaced plants such as squashes or tomatoes). Scatter the fertilizer evenly in the trench, cover it with soil, and water. For small gardens and container crops, apply liquid fertilizers with a watering can or hose-end sprayer.

Side-dressing dry fertilizer

Trench 4" from plants

Liquid fertilizer mixture

Mulch around plants

Mulching controls weed growth, retains soil moisture, protects soil from erosion, reduces soil compaction, keeps produce and leaves clean, and provides a barrier between plants and soilborne diseases. Mulches can also harbor pests, so keep an eye out for them. For established plants, apply organic mulches such as sawdust, straw, ground bark, compost, or well-rotted manure 2 to 4 inches thick. Use less material in wet climates and more in dry climates.

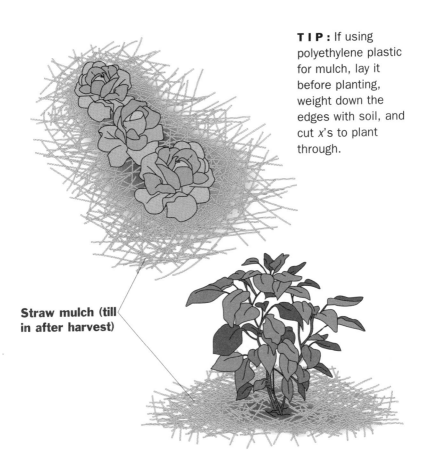

TIP: If using polyethylene plastic for mulch, lay it before planting, weight down the edges with soil, and cut *x*'s to plant through.

Straw mulch (till in after harvest)

Stake and support

Put up stakes, poles, trellises, and other supports at planting time. Train or tie the plants as they grow. Don't use metal in hot climates—new growth can be burned. Stake tomato plants to wood or bamboo poles, or support them within wire cages. Other vegetables can be staked with PVC pipe, bamboo, poles, or 2×2s. Supports can be built on a flat plane or in the shape of a teepee or A-frame. Vines can be trained along a fence at the edge of the garden or on trellises made of fishing line or string.

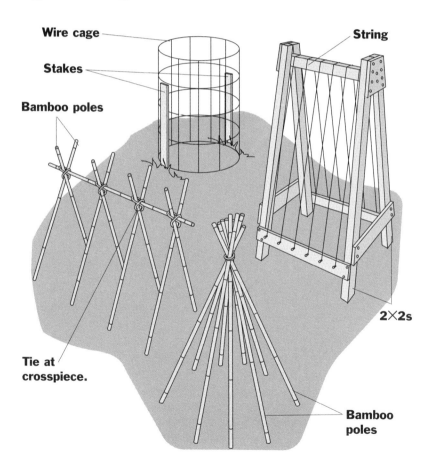

Wire cage

String

Stakes

Bamboo poles

Tie at crosspiece.

2×2s

Bamboo poles

 Control pests

One way to avoid problems is to choose vegetable varieties genetically designed to resist pests. Do not buy transplants that show symptoms of insect damage. Healthy, vigorous plants can withstand light pest attacks, so create the best growing environment above and below ground. At least once a week, check leaves, flowers, and stems for signs of harmful insects. (Identify insects correctly—many are helpful.) Clear out plant debris and weeds in and around the garden.

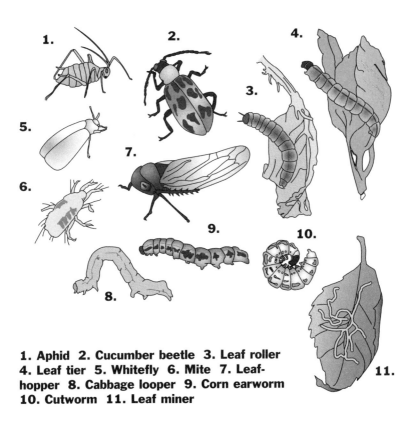

1. Aphid 2. Cucumber beetle 3. Leaf roller 4. Leaf tier 5. Whitefly 6. Mite 7. Leaf-hopper 8. Cabbage looper 9. Corn earworm 10. Cutworm 11. Leaf miner

Note: Pests are not drawn to scale.

You can mail-order some beneficial insects to keep harmful pests at bay. Insecticidal soap can also be used. Hand-pick and dispose of large pests such as caterpillars, snails, or tomato hornworms. Eliminate small pests such as aphids with a jet of water from the hose. Take stronger measures only if your first efforts fail. When using insecticides on vegetables, read labels carefully and follow directions exactly. Be sure the product is safe for edible crops. The label will tell you which plants you can spray and how long to wait before harvesting.

Beneficial Insects

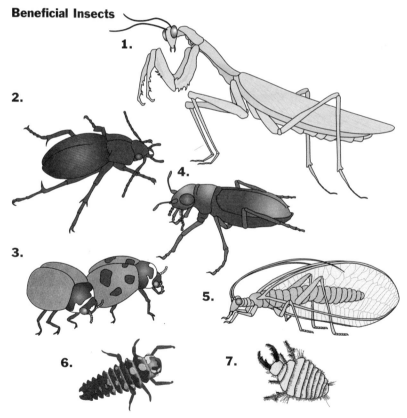

1. Praying mantis 2. Ground beetle 3. Ladybird beetles
4. Tiger beetle 5. Lacewing 6. Ladybird beetle larva
7. Lacewing larva

7 Prevent diseases

Planting disease-resistant varieties is one of the best means to a healthy garden. Tomatoes labeled *VFN* are one example—this means they resist verticillium wilt, fusarium wilt, and nematodes. Avoid watering late in the day to prevent leaves from being wet for extended cool periods, which is when fungal spores germinate and spread. Don't work among wet plants; this enables disease-causing organisms to spread from plant to plant. Avoid crowding plants, which can limit air circulation. Poorly drained soil also contributes to fungal diseases. Keep

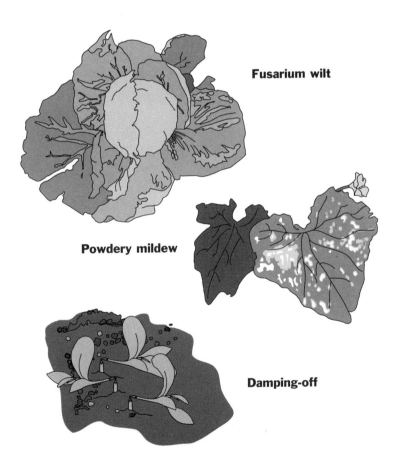

Fusarium wilt

Powdery mildew

Damping-off

weeds from growing, and control aphids and other insects, as they can spread viral diseases.

Some soilborne diseases can be controlled by rotating crops within the garden so that plants of a common family aren't grown in the same area year after year. If needed, fungicides developed specifically for vegetables can be used to keep infections from getting started, or right after the disease is first observed to prevent it from spreading. Reapply if it rains heavily soon after you have sprayed the plants.

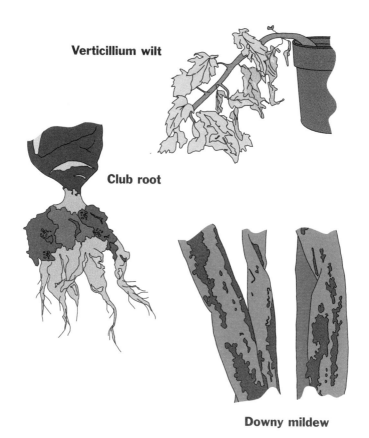

Verticillium wilt

Club root

Downy mildew

Deter animals and birds

To keep gophers and moles from damaging crops, plant in raised beds or in-ground beds lined with heavy-duty chicken wire; or make individual mesh baskets to protect plant roots. A 2-foot-high fence of 1½-inch mesh should keep rabbits out. Secure the bottom with 12 inches folded outward underground and staked or weighted down to prevent burrowing. Use a strand of electric fencing on top as an added deterrent. To prevent cats from digging in newly tilled soil, lay chicken wire or hardware cloth over the seedbed until plants sprout.

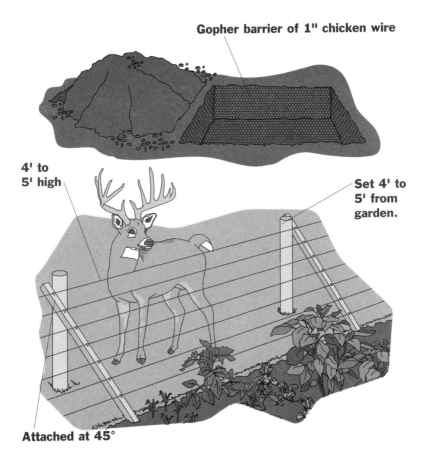

Gopher barrier of 1" chicken wire

4' to 5' high

Set 4' to 5' from garden.

Attached at 45°

A 4- to 5-foot-tall fence slanted outward at a 45-degree angle will keep out deer—they are less likely to jump a wide fence. A vertical fence would have to be at least 8 feet high. Deer repellents, such as bags of human hair hung along the garden perimeter or dried blood (as in blood meal fertilizer) sprinkled on the ground, can also be used but must be renewed frequently and always after rain. To keep out mice and birds, protect individual plants or rows of seedlings with an enclosed tent of chicken wire or plastic mesh.

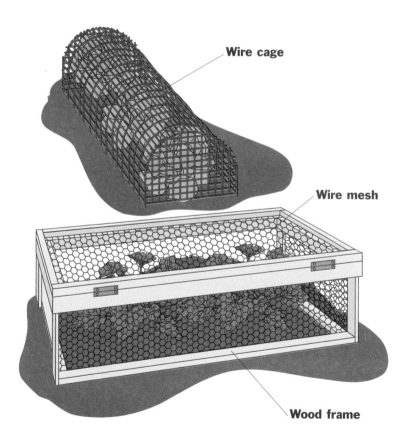

Wire cage

Wire mesh

Wood frame

Increasing the Harvest

Stagger planting times

Stretch the harvest period by staggering the planting of seeds or transplants at roughly one- to two-week intervals. For example, if you plant lettuce in mid-March, you can plant more in late March, mid-April, and late April. Successive plantings of snap beans four to six weeks apart will provide fresh beans for five months or more. You can also select varieties of a similar crop that mature at different rates. Some crops such as beets and carrots provide a succession of harvests. Begin when they are baby-sized and continue up to maturity.

Make successive plantings.

T I P : Radishes and green onions grow so quickly that you can raise a second crop in the same spot after the first is harvested.

2 Protect with row covers

Use row covers to start your garden earlier and prolong your fall harvest. Made from fabric or transparent plastic, they provide from 2° to 7° F of frost protection. The lightweight fabric allows water, light, and air in, but keeps most insects out. Vent plastic covers—slit the plastic or roll it up during the day to prevent overheating. Plastic or fabric can be stretched over and connected to wire hoops or wood frames. Remove when the danger of frost has passed or the plants are well established.

Plastic over wood frame

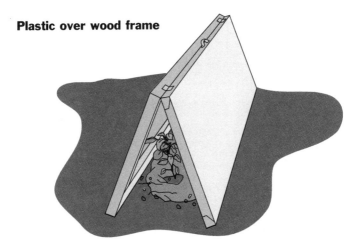

Row cover

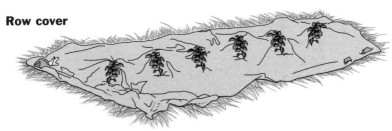

3

Use cloches and hot caps

Protect individual plants from frost with cloches. Use plastic milk jugs with the bottoms cut out and the tops left open during the day, or make cone-shaped cloches, 18 inches in diameter or larger, from fiberglass-reinforced plastic or polyethylene pulled over wooden supports. Make sure the covering allows for adequate light and ventilation. Garden-supply catalogs and stores offer several choices of cloches. Remove them when the plants are well established.

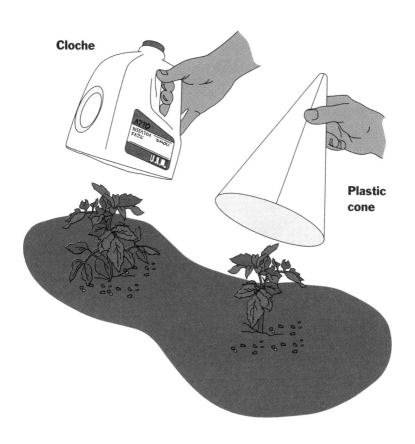

Cloche

Plastic cone

4 Build cold frames or hotbeds

Made of redwood or pressure-treated lumber, a cold frame is a bottomless box for capturing and retaining solar heat. Put it in a sunny spot. It can be portable or permanently embedded in the ground. It is covered with a slanted and hinged window that should face the south and away from prevailing winds. Use it to toughen tender transplants or seedlings started indoors and to grow cold-tolerant crops. When the temperature drops below 32° F, cover the frame with a tarp, carpeting, or a sheet of styrene foam. On warm days, prop open the roof.

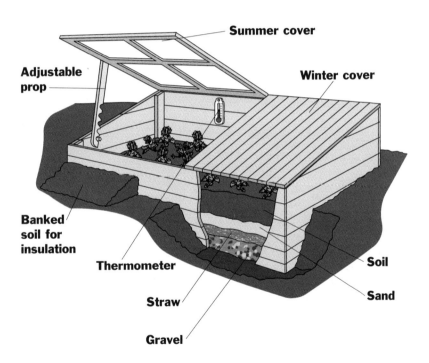

Summer cover

Adjustable prop

Winter cover

Banked soil for insulation

Thermometer

Straw

Gravel

Soil

Sand

A hotbed is a cold frame with buried electric cables to heat the soil and plants, causing seeds to germinate early and quickly. You can sow seeds directly in the soil above the cables and raise cool-season crops when it is too cold to plant outdoors. Spread a 2-inch layer of sand, loop the covered cable on the sand, and cover with ½-inch wire mesh. If you will place containers in the hotbed, spread 2 inches of sand over the mesh. To plant directly in the hotbed, cover the mesh with a 4-inch layer of potting soil instead of sand.

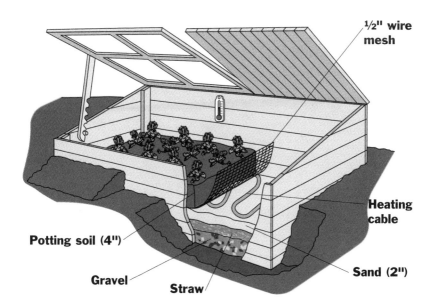

½" wire mesh

Heating cable

Potting soil (4")

Sand (2")

Gravel

Straw

 Know when to pick

Check your planting record for expected dates of maturity and start inspecting a week early. It is best to pick in the morning while vegetables are still cool but after dew has dried. Taste a few to test for readiness. Many crops are best harvested before they reach full size. A 14-inch zucchini is impressive, but smaller ones taste better. Frequent harvests prolong the productive life span of most plants. For "baby" vegetables, pick every day. Harvest crops just before you plan to eat or preserve them.

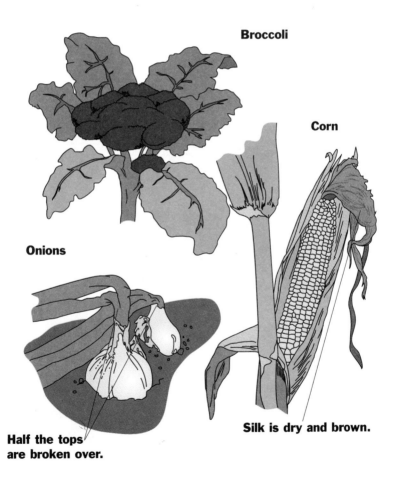

Broccoli

Corn

Onions

Silk is dry and brown.

Half the tops are broken over.

Harvest with care

When you head to the garden to harvest, bring a sharp harvesting knife, bags or buckets, and maybe a wire basket for easily washing produce with a hose. Don't harvest when plants are wet, especially beans. Many fungus diseases spread in moist conditions, and brushing the plants can carry disease organisms down the row. Harvest early in the day when moisture and sugar levels are highest. Pick produce carefully to avoid bruising. To prevent injuring root crops, use a spading fork rather than a shovel.

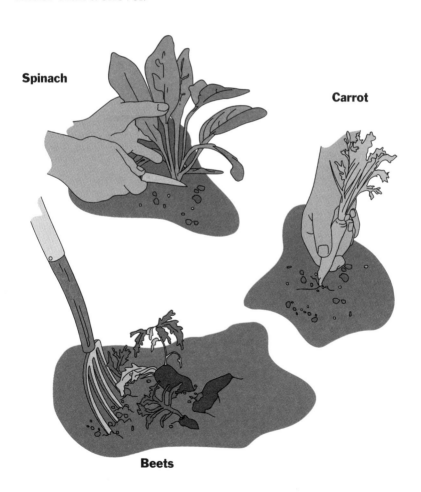

Spinach

Carrot

Beets

More Information

Harvest Guide

Here are harvesting tips for some popular vegetables:

Artichokes   Harvest when the flower buds are 4 inches across and before they start to open. Cut the stems, retaining a piece, with a knife or pruning shears.

Beans   Pick when the sides of the pods are just starting to bulge. Green (snap) beans should snap when you break them, and pods shouldn't be stringy. Pick limas when beans are plump and green (not white). Pick dry beans after pods have yellowed but before they begin to shatter.

Beets   Harvest when they are 2 to 3 inches across. Gently poke your finger into the soil around the beet to check its size before pulling. Use thinned-out greens and roots for salads.

Broccoli   Harvest the center flower bud cluster while the green buds are still tight and before there is any yellow showing.

Cabbage   Begin harvesting when heads are firm and glossy and about the size of a softball. Cut just below the head, leaving some basal leaves to support the growth of small lateral heads.

Carrots   Eat thinned-out carrots anytime. Harvest the main crop of medium-sized varieties when their tops are ¾ to 1½ inches across.

Cauliflower   As the curds (the white part that you eat) reach silver-dollar size, tie their leaves over them to prevent sunburn. Cut beneath the top set of leaves when the head is 4 to 6 inches across, white, and solid.

Celery   Dig the whole plant from the ground or pull off and eat the outer stalks, leaving the inner stalks to grow.

Chard   Start picking the outer leaves when they are young and tender, after plants reach 6 to 8 inches in height.

Corn   As the silk tassels begin to wither and turn brown, open a husk and press a kernel. If it spurts milky juice, it is ready to pick. Hold the ear at its base and bend it downward in a twisting motion.

Cucumbers   Pick slicing cucumbers when they are 7 to 8 inches long, pickling cucumbers when they are 3 to 6 inches long. Cut them off the vine with a knife or shears to prevent breaking the stem. Harvest lemon cucumbers before they are 3 inches in diameter.

Eggplant   Select fruit that has a high gloss and pick when young. Push on the side of the fruit with the ball of your thumb; if the indentation does not spring back, the fruit is mature.

Lettuce   Pick leaf types when outer leaves are 4 to 6 inches long. Harvest head types when heads are moderately firm, before flower stalks appear.

Onions   Harvest bulbed varieties by pulling them from the ground when half of the tops have broken over naturally. Once out of the ground, cut the tops off 1½ inches above the bulb when they have fully wilted. Chives can be clipped almost continuously, and leeks harvested in the fall anytime after the leaves are ¾ inch wide.

Peas   Pick English peas when pods are plump and dark green. Harvest edible-pod kinds (snow and Chinese) before seeds start to bulge the pod wall. Harvest snap peas when pods are plump.

Peppers   Bell peppers are usually picked green and immature but full sized and firm; if they ripen on the plant, they will be sweeter and higher in vitamins. Chiles are picked at full maturity.

Potatoes   Pick new potatoes as soon as the tops flower. For full-sized tubers, wait until the vines yellow or die back. To avoid bruising them, loosen the soil with a rake or a spading fork first, then dig them up. Do not wash the potatoes before storing them—just brush off any dirt.

Radishes   Pull when 1½ inches in diameter.

Spinach   Harvest when leaves are 6 to 8 inches long and before the plant begins to flower. Cut and eat the outer leaves for a continuing supply, or pull the entire plant.

Squash   Pick winter squash before frost when the fruits are hard. Harvest summer squash when fruits are young, tender, and about as long as your hand.

Tomatoes   For the best flavor and maximum sugar content, leave fruit on the vine an extra day after they have turned completely red. Green tomatoes will ripen indoors on a windowsill, or they can be cooked while still green.

Planting Chart

Many of the vegetables listed below can be sown indoors or in a cold frame and later transplanted to the garden, or they can be purchased as transplants from a reputable nursery. The "Weeks to grow to transplant size" column indicates the number of weeks the seeds need after sowing indoors, in a cold frame, or in a greenhouse until the plants are large enough to be moved to the garden.

Vegetable	Depth to plant seed	Number of seeds to sow per foot	Distance between plants	Days to germination	Weeks to grow to transplant size	Days to maturity
Artichoke	½"	—	60"	7–14	4–6*	12 mos.
Arugula	¼"	8–10	8"–12"	7–14	—	60
Asparagus	1½"	—	18"	7–21	12–14*	3 years
Asparagus bean, or yard-long bean	½"–1"	2–4	12"–24"	6–13	—	65–80
Bean						
Snap bush	1"–1½"	6–8	2"–3"	6–14	—	45–65
Snap pole	1"–1½"	4–6	4"–6"	6–14	—	60–70
Lima bush	1½"–2"	5–8	3"–6"	7–12	—	60–80
Lima pole	1½"–2"	4–5	6"–10"	7–12	—	85–90
Garbanzo, or chick-pea	1½"–2"	5–8	3"–4"	6–12	—	105
Scarlet runner	1"–1½"	4–6	4"–6"	6–14	—	60–70
Soy bean	1½"–2"	6–8	2"–3"	6–14	—	55–85
Beet[2]	½"–1"	10–15	2"	7–10	—	55–65
Black-eyed pea, cowpea, or southern pea	½"–1"	5–8	3"–4"	7–10	—	65–80
Broccoli	½"	10–15	14"–18"	3–10	5–7*	60–80T

* Transplants preferred over seed.
T Number of days from setting out transplants; others are from seeding.
[2] Use thinnings for early greens.

Vegetable	Depth to plant seed	Number of seeds to sow per foot	Distance between plants	Days to germination	Weeks to grow to transplant size	Days to maturity
Brussels sprouts	½"	10–15	12"–18"	3–10	4–6*	80–90T
Cabbage	½"	8–10	12"–20"	4–10	5–7*	65–95T
Cabbage Chinese	½"	8–10	10"–12"	4–10	4–6	80–90
Cardoon	½"	4–6	18"	8–14	8	120–150
Carrot[3]	¼"	15–20	1"–2"	10–17	—	60–80
Cauliflower	½"	8–10	18"	4–10	5–7*	55–65T
Celeriac	⅛"	8–12	8"	9–21	10–12*	90–120T
Celery	⅛"	8–12	8"	9–21	10–12*	90–120T
Celtuce	½"	8–10	12"	4–10	4–6	80
Chard, Swiss[2]	1"	6–10	4"–8"	7–10	—	55–65
Chicory	¼"	8–10	4"–8"	5–12	—	90–120
Chives	½"	8–10	8"	8–12	6–8	80–90
Collards	¼"	10–12	10"–15"	4–10	4–6*	65–85T
Corn, sweet	2"	4–6	10"–14"	6–10	—	60–90
Cress, garden	¼"	10–12	2"–3"	4–10	—	24–45
Cucumber	1"	3–5	12"	6–10	4	55–65
Eggplant	¼"–½"	8–12	18"	7–14	6–9*	75–95T
Endive	½"	4–6	9"–12"	5–9	4–6	60–90
Fennel, Florence	½"	8–12	6"	6–17	—	120

* Transplants preferred over seed.
T Number of days from setting out transplants; others are from seeding.
[2] Use thinnings for early greens.
[3] Start using when ½" in diameter to thin rows.

Planting Chart (continued)

Vegetable	Depth to plant seed	Number of seeds to sow per foot	Distance between plants	Days to germination	Weeks to grow to transplant size	Days to maturity
Garlic (bulb)	1"	—	2"–4"	6–10	—	90, sets
Ground cherry, or husk tomato	½"	6	24"	6–13	6*	90–100T
Jerusalem artichoke	4"⁴	—	15"–24"	—	—	100–105
Jicama	¼"	—	6"–8"	7	2	4–8 mos.
Kale	½"	8–12	8"–12"	3–10	4–6	55–80
Kohlrabi	½"	8–12	8"–12"	3–10	4–6	60–70
Leek	½"–1"	8–12	2"–4"	7–12	10–12*	80–90T
Lettuce, head	¼"–½"	4–8	12"–14"	4–10	3–5*	55–80
Lettuce, leaf	¼"–½"	8–12	4"–6"	4–10	3–5	45–60
Muskmelon	1"	3–6	12"	4–8	3–4	75–100
Mustard	½"	8–10	2"–6"	3–10	—	40–60
Nasturtium	½"–1"	4–8	4"–10"	—	—	50–60
Okra	1"	6–8	15"–18"	7–14	4–6	50–60
Onion, sets	1"–2"	—	2"–3"	—	—	95–120
Onion, plants	2"–3"	—	2"–3"	—	8	95–120T
Onion, seed	½"	10–15	2"–3"	7–12	—	100–165
Parsnip	½"	8–12	3"–4"	15–25	—	100–120
Pea	2"	6–7	2"–3"	6–15	—	65–85
Pepper	¼"	6–8	18"–24"	10–20	6–8*	60–80T
Potato	4"⁴	1	12"	8–16	—	90–105

* Transplants preferred over seed.
T Number of days from setting out transplants; others are from seeding.
⁴ Tubers

Vegetable	Depth to plant seed	Number of seeds to sow per foot	Distance between plants	Days to germination	Weeks to grow to transplant size	Days to maturity
Pumpkin	1"–1½"	2	30"	6–10	—	70–110
Radicchio	¼"	4–5	8"–10"	5–12	—	80–110
Radish	½"	14–16	1"–2"	3–10	—	20–50
Rutabaga	½"	4–6	8"–12"	3–10	—	80–90
Salsify	½"	8–12	2"–3"	—	—	110–150
Salsify, black	½"	8–12	2"–3"	—	—	110–150
Shallot, bulb	1"	—	2"–4"	—	—	60–75
Sorrel	⅛"	4	10"	10	—	100
Spinach	½"	10–12	2"–4"	6–14	—	40–65
Malabar	½"	4–6	12"	10	6–8*	70
New Zealand	1½"	4–6	18"	5–10	—	70–80
Tampala	¼"–½"	6–10	4"–6"	—	—	21–42
Squash, summer	1"	4–6	16"–24"	3–12	3–4	50–60
Squash, winter	1"	1–2	24"–48"	6–10	3–4	85–120
Sweet potato	plants	—	12"–18"	—	—	120
Tomatillo	½"	6	24"	6–13	6	90–100T
Tomato	½"	—	18"–36"	6–14	5–7*	55–90T
Turnip[2]	½"	14–16	1"–3"	3–10	—	45–60
Watermelon	1"	—	12"–16"	3–12	—	80–100

* Transplants preferred over seed.
T Number of days from setting out transplants; others are from seeding.
[2] Use thinnings for early greens.

Storage Recommendations

Store vegetables at the right temperature and relative humidity to maintain quality and nutritive value. Most produce needs to be cleaned before storing, with the excess water thoroughly drained off. Vegetables being stored under dry conditions (garlic, onions, winter squash) should be wiped clean of dirt but not washed. Vegetables stored in the refrigerator should be placed in plastic bags or containers.

Vegetable	Temperature	Humidity	Storage Period (app.)
Cold, Moist Storage			
Asparagus	32°–35° F	85–90%	2–3 weeks
Beet, topped	32° F	95%	3–5 months
Broccoli	32°–35° F	90–95%	10–14 days
Brussels sprout	32°–35° F	90–95%	3–5 weeks ·
Cabbage, Chinese	32° F	90–95%	1–2 months
Cabbage, late	32° F	90–95%	3–4 months
Carrot, mature/topped	32°–35° F	90–95%	4–5 months
Cauliflower	32°–35° F	85–90%	2–4 weeks
Celeriac	32° F	90–95%	3–4 months
Celery	32°–35° F	90–95%	2–3 months
Collards	32°–35° F	90–95%	10–14 days
Corn, sweet	32°–35° F	85–90%	4–8 days
Endive, escarole	32° F	90–95%	2–3 weeks
Greens, leafy	32° F	90–95%	10–14 days
Horseradish	30–33° F	90–95%	10–12 months
Kale	32° F	90–95%	10–14 days
Kohlrabi	32° F	90–95%	2–4 weeks
Leek, green	32° F	90–95%	1–3 months
Lettuce	32°–35° F	90–95%	2–3 weeks
Onion, green	32°–35° F	90–95%	3–4 weeks
Parsnip	32°–35° F	90–95%	2–6 months
Pea	35–40° F	85–90%	1–3 weeks
Potato, late crop	35–40° F	85–90%	4–9 months
Radish	32°–35° F	90–95%	3–4 weeks
Rhubarb	32°–35° F	90–95%	2–4 weeks

Vegetable	Temperature	Humidity	Storage Period (app.)
Cold, Moist Storage (continued)			
Rutabaga	32°–35° F	90–95%	2–4 months
Spinach	32°–35° F	90–95%	10–14 days
Turnip	32° F	90–95%	4–5 months
Cool, Moist Storage			
Bean, snap	40°–45° F	90–95%	7–10 days
Bean, lima	32°–40° F	90%	1–2 weeks
Cantaloupe	40° F	90%	15 days
Cucumber	40°–50° F	85–90%	10–14 days
Eggplant	40°–50° F	85–90%	1 week
Okra	45° F	90–95%	7–10 days
Pepper, bell	40°–50° F	85–90%	2–3 weeks
Potato, early	50° F	90%	1–3 weeks
Potato, late	40° F	90%	4–9 months
Squash, summer	40°–50° F	90%	5–14 days
Tomato, ripe	40°–50° F	85–90%	4–7 days
Tomato, unripe	60°–70° F	85–90%	1–3 weeks
Watermelon	40°–50° F	80–85%	2–3 weeks
Cool, Dry Storage			
Bean, dried	32°–40° F	40%	Over 1 year
Chile, dried	32°–50° F	60–70%	6 months
Garlic, dried	32° F	65–70%	6–7 months
Onion, dried	32° F	65–70%	1–8 months
Pea, dried	32°–40° F	40%	Over 1 year
Shallot, dried	32° F	60–70%	6–7 months
Warm, Dry Storage			
Pumpkin	55°–65° F	40–70%	2–4 months
Squash, winter	55°–65° F	40–70%	3–6 months
Sweet potato	55°–60° F	70–85%	4–6 months

Freezing Vegetables

To freeze vegetables, select firm, unblemished crops and wash them well with cold water. Blanch by submerging them in boiling water for 1 to 4 minutes, depending on the vegetable. Then cool them by rinsing under running tap water. Dry them with a towel and place in freezer bags, freezer jars, or plastic freezer containers. When closed, such containers should be moisture-proof.

Vegetable	Suitability for Freezing	Comments
Asparagus	Excellent	Select young stalks with compact tips.
Bean, green	Good	Tendercrop and related varieties and Blue Lake varieties, either bush or pole, are preferred because of their good flavor. Also, Blue Lake varieties have a desirable thick flesh.
Bean, lima	Excellent	Fordhook types preferred.
Bean, wax	Good	
Beet	Fair	Better canned; select only small roots for freezing.
Broccoli	Excellent	
Cabbage	Not recommended	Preserve as sauerkraut.
Carrot	Fair	Select tender roots only. Can be diced and frozen with peas.
Cauliflower	Excellent	Also suitable for pickling.
Celery	Not recommended	Except for soup.
Corn, sweet	Good to excellent	'Jubilee', 'Seneca Chief', 'Golden Cross', and 'Silver Queen' preferred; corn on the cob frozen without blanching should be eaten in 6–8 weeks.
Cucumber	Not recommended	
Eggplant	Fair	Significant quality loss*; suitable for casseroles.
Endive	Not recommended	
Kale	Good	Select young leaves only.
Lettuce	Not recommended	

Vegetable	Suitability for Freezing	Comments*
Muskmelon	Fair	Firm-fleshed varieties are preferred; freeze small pieces; use within 3 months.
Mustard	Good	Select tender leaves and remove stems.
Onion	Fair	Freeze chopped, mature onions; significant quality lossfrozen; use in 3 months.
Pea	Excellent	All large, wrinkled-seeded varieties are suitable; so are edible-pod varieties.
Pepper	Fair	Significant quality loss*; better if frozen chopped; use in 3 months.
Popcorn	Not recommended	Store dry.
Potato	Not recommended	Store fresh at 40°–50° F.
Rhubarb	Excellent	Varieties with red stalks, such as 'Canada Red', 'Valentine', and 'Ruby', preferred.
Spinach	Excellent	Savoy varieties are often preferred.
Squash, summer	Fair	Significant quality loss*.
Squash, winter	Good	Be sure that squash is fully mature (hard rind); freeze cooked pieces or mash.
Swiss chard	Good	Select only tender leaves; remove midribs and stems.
Tomato	Fair	Better canned; freeze only juice or cooked tomatoes.
Turnip & rutabaga	Fair	Significant quality loss*.
Watermelon	Fair	Freeze only as pieces; use within 3 months.

Significant quality loss means that the product after being frozen is quite inferior to the fresh product.

Chart adapted from Roth Klippstein and P. A. Minges, Home Garden Dept. of Vegetable Crops, Cornell University.

U.S./Metric Measure Conversions

Formulas for Exact Measures

	Symbol	When you know:	Multiply by:	To find:
Mass (Weight)	oz	ounces	28.35	grams
	lb	pounds	0.45	kilograms
	g	grams	0.035	ounces
	kg	kilograms	2.2	pounds
Volume	pt	pints	0.47	liters
	qt	quarts	0.95	liters
	gal	gallons	3.785	liters
	ml	milliliters	0.034	fluid ounces
Length	in.	inches	2.54	centimeters
	ft	feet	30.48	centimeters
	yd	yards	0.9144	meters
	mi	miles	1.609	kilometers
	km	kilometers	0.621	miles
	m	meters	1.094	yards
	cm	centimeters	0.39	inches
Temperature	° F	Fahrenheit	5/9 (after subtracting 32)	Celsius
	° C	Celsius	9/5 (then add 32)	Fahrenheit
Area	in.^{2}	square inches	6.452	square centimeters
	ft^2	square feet	929.0	square centimeters
	yd^2	square yards	8361.0	square centimeters
	a.	acres	0.4047	hectares

Rounded Measures for Quick Reference

1 oz	= 30 g
4 oz	= 115 g
8 oz	= 225 g
16 oz = 1 lb	= 450 g
32 oz = 2 lb	= 900 g
36 oz = 2$^1/_4$ lb	= 1000 g (1 kg)
1 c	= 250 ml
2 c (1pt)	= 500 ml
4 c (1 qt)	= 1 liter
4 qt (1 gal)	= 3$^3/_4$ liter
$^3/_8$ in.	= 1.0 cm
1 in.	= 2.5 cm
2 in.	= 5.0 cm
2$^1/_2$ in.	= 6.5 cm
12 in. (1 ft)	= 30.0 cm
1 yd	= 90.0 cm
100 ft	= 30.0 m
1 mi	= 1.6 km
32° F	= 0° C
212° F	= 100° C
1 in.^{2}	= 6.5 cm^2
1 ft^2	= 930 cm^2
1 yd^2	= 8360 cm^2
1 a.	= 4050 m^2